Stomp and Sing

poems by

JON ANDERSEN

CURBSTONE PRESS

Printed in the U.S. on acid-free paper by BookMobile

Cover design: Stone Graphics
Cover artwork © Kerri Quirk

 This book was published with the support of the
Connecticut Commission on Culture and Tourism,
and donations from many individuals. We are very
grateful for this support.

Connecticut Commission
on Culture & Tourism

Library of Congress Cataloging-in-Publication Data

Andersen, Jon, 1970-
  Stomp and sing : poems / by Jon Andersen.— 1st ed.
     p. cm.
  ISBN 1-931896-15-1 (pbk. : acid-free paper)
  1. Working class—Poetry. 2. Working class families—Poetry. I.
Title.
  PS3601.N435S76 2005
  811'.6—°dc22

                    2004029791

published by
  CURBSTONE PRESS   321 Jackson Street   Willimantic, CT 06226
          phone: 860-423-5110   e-mail: info@curbstone.org
                  http://www.curbstone.org

Grateful acknowledgment is made to the editors of the following journals in which many of these poems, some in different forms, have previously appeared or are forthcoming:

Blue Collar Review, The Café Review, Connecticut Review, Crushed Cigarette Press, The Hartford Courant, Haight-Ashbury Literary Journal, Haz Mat Review, In Our Own Words, Pemmican, The Pittsburgh Quarterly, Poetry Motel, The Progressive and *Rattle.*

"My Mother Paints Again" appeared in *O Taste and See: Food Poems* (Bottom Dog Press 2003). Winner of the American Poetry Anthology Award.

"Encounter" was featured in a limited edition lithograph series by the artist Andy Green.

"Green World" was awarded the 2004 People Before Profits Poetry Prize (Burning Bush Books)

"F.Y.I." was published in a limited broadside series at Curbstone Press (March 2004)

I owe a deep debt of gratitude to the members of my writing group whose advice in crafting these poems and this book has been essential: James Coleman, Joan Joffe Hall, Alison Meyers, David Morse, and Denise Abercrombie.

Thanks also to Judith Aubrecht, Christopher Gazzola, Kate Martin, and Steve Pozzato, who provided very helpful critiques of an early draft; to James Scully, who was the right teacher at the right time; to the late Leo Connellan, who delivered gruff and generous lectures over the phone; and to Alexander Taylor and Judith Doyle, who believed in and supported this work.

CONTENTS

III. The Real World

for Denise, Miles, and Kit

STOMP and SING

I.

Fierce to Go

The Mulberry Tree

Cats wait. An August orgy, a squawking and fluttering feast
swells the fissured limbs of the mulberry tree—
the moral tree Nanny calls it. Starlings and robins

fight for spots among the saw-toothed waxy leaves, dart
for beakfuls of the dark fruit hanging from the highest branches.
I am five years old and I watch a blue jay stumble drunk along

the tar paper peak of the tilting summer kitchen, wobble,
drop. Laughing at the slapstick, I run over to where it flops
in the lavender ajuga carpet at the base of the tree.

I stand over the silly bird, my white sneakers stained blood-red
with fermenting berries. The jay gawks and rolls a little, one
awkward wing flaps ridiculously—this *is* funny! But a funny

kind of funny. I giggle, but my belly feels like it did
when I ran into the Rustic Café one morning and found
an old man curled up on the bar, snoring like some fantastic beast.

The Street Named After Spencer

On I-384 East, headed back
to my wife and children
I pass the Spencer Street Exit

and my brother and I are treed like a couple of bear cubs
by two Dobermans on military property
when here comes our buddy Spencer
rattling down the road on some bike he's cobbled together,
laughing and yelling like a lunatic
swinging his daddy's nightstick.

Moments later it seems
we're all getting through high school
and Spencer's standing outside my honors English class
having skipped out of auto shop to tell me
how he values our friendship
cutting across precious literature read aloud with
"Hey, Andersen, you suck!"

I see him cry again that one time—no
outright sobbing, just a few angry tears
one night as the whole gang of us
sprawls in the back of Jim Mingo's van
drinking beer: he admits
that his black eye, his broken nose
wasn't no motorcycle accident
but something "War Hawk" gave him:
"My old man's only got three fingers on his right
and, boy, that's the one you've got to watch out for"
but he just can't seem to see any way out…
then starts to laugh, asks: "Your folks are cool—
think they could afford to feed me?"
"No way. Not unless they trade me in," I answer

before waking up at the end of this highway
that drops me off into my new life,
where I am wondering at and grateful for
whatever part of us it is
that navigates across so many miles, delivers us
safe, and if we're lucky, whole.

Spencer's Scrapbook

In the black,
Spencer clutches his mother's hand,
terrified as they walk the low orchard rows
and call out: *Grampa! Gramps!*

Aunt June turns on the light in the barn,
looks up into the rafters.

By the time Officer Smith's cruiser spotlight
slips across the honeysuckle tangle and tumble
of stonewall along Whistletown Road

Grampa George is three hours into a whiskey rage
and up to his waist in Lake Pattagansett
thrashing the black water
crying and hollering out to his dead wife
Agnes! Agnes! Agnes! only
his own voice answering him, calling him farther out
towards the spill of moonlight in the clouds.

Daddy wheels into the boat launch just in time,
finds and drags his son-of-a-bitch father from the water,
roughs him up just enough to feel good
about leaving the broken old man blubbering
and stinking of lake muck in the back of the station wagon
as he stops in Flanders for cigarettes on the way home.

Civilian Life: 1976

*All the peoples on the earth are equal from birth, all the peoples have a
right to live, to be happy and free.* — Ho Chi Minh, 1945

When blossoms float in morning sun
my father runs from chore to chore
humming like tripwire—
                now sprung—
now strung back taut and tense again—
he's angry as artillery,
he's fixing broken mowers, tools,
he's cursing endless Sunday tasks.

I've chosen to accept my mission
to photograph the enemy;
I crawl and sneak around the side
of our little farmhouse—our home:
six years ago an empty shack
still haunted by the clammy ghosts
of crazy kin. My parents worked
and made a little paradise....

But now we hear and feel the blasts.
The tattered sound of M-16s
shredding another sunny day
scatters from up on old Stone's Ranch
(about a quarter mile straight-shot
through swamps and woods—a training site
for drunken *weekend warriors*).

Choppers lift off, one swoops
into this valley pounding sky—apple
boughs snap and dirt rips up in clumps
that burst, blow out across the fields
and yards. I dare to peek around

the corner of the house. A good
soldier, I stifle sniggers, crouch
and wait. He turns about, marches
right towards my hiding place. I clutch
my mother's camera and advance
the film; he bends down for a sledge—

I rise up like a sniper, snap
the shot; watch—awestruck as he steps
out of that flash of sudden light
as if to dance, but twists, stops short—
he jerks, half-
            turns, leaps for his life—
his life—down open bulkhead doors.

Hi-Fi

Years before my parents' divorce
I could just keep pace with my father
on his one day off a week—tending
garden, clearing land, making things
work. Only rain, driving against our old house
in waves, could transform Sunday into a day of rest.
My father stacked albums on his turntable, smoked
Belairs, listened with anticipation through the hum of the amp
and the dust crackling as the stylus dropped. I'd tackle
one of his old paperbacks: *The Great Gatsby*,
Catch-22, *Hiroshima*, and stop at notes scribbled
in the margins before I was born (*so much left to do*—
LIFE! scrawled in his hard blue script across a yellow page
of Gunther's *Death Be Not Proud*). Then blasting through
the system he bought for himself after the war,
with *perfect balance, highest brilliance,* and *purest*
definition, rose the hi-fi crashing Sousa Marches,
the desperate hard rock tenor of Judas
in *Jesus Christ Superstar,* or the sweet, rich voice
of Harry Belafonte. My Dad, red-faced and laughing,
would grab me with his long arms, wrestle me to the rug,
the second floor shaking with our roughhousing
and the stereo blaring:
daylight come and me want to go home....

Green World

*Groton, Connecticut—"The Submarine Capital of the World"—sits at the
mouth of the Thames River and is home to the Electric Boat Shipyard, which
has for many years produced nuclear submarines for the United States Navy*

I mow endless swatches of lawn
in the *Submarine Capital of the World*;
even just walking back to the truck to grab my lunch
I continue to make zero turns
and float an invisible deck. My ears roar,
my hands stick in such a grip
that I must look like a strangler. Still…

it *is* peaceful sitting on the wall above the sidewalk—
people file into Paul's Pasta across the street;
a dark-haired, full-lipped girl looks into my eyes
for a split second as she slips by laughing
in a yellow convertible; one flamboyant punk—
tall and bent like a nail—leans against a pole and smokes;
pipe fitters and carpenters stride like Greek heroes
down to another shift at *The Boat*. I taste peanut butter
and jelly and grass clippings, listen to the block
and tackle ringing out from tall ships—one sloop
half-sunk at its dock—and watch
a graceful Trident slicing through the Thames.

(Which reminds me of War Hawk, the scars on his back
he got from squatting down in the missile tubes
to finish welds that dripped and seared the flesh, trapping him
in a chamber of sparks and chorus of his own screams.
Just last week he really let me have it: *Protesting?*
You college kids are the dumbest! There'd be no one
paying you or your Dad to mow lawns without the subs—
I promise you that! and then lay down on the hot pavement
to finish welding the patch on my truck for free).

10

Now I hear the bells sounds in salt air, watch
the graceful cut through the Thames of a Trident
plowing towards the deep North Atlantic: a sleek
gun-metal Leviathan carrying sun-hot fire in its belly
burning like a billion acetylene torches

or burning like the hope I tend:
that somehow we will find a way,
somehow, we will find a way to go back
on this promise we've all helped to make:

the end of the whole green world

The Lumberyard Needs a Real Nigger

Can you lift shit, can you take shit,
can you do what I say, boy? Cause
what we need is a real nigger around here....
My first interview and I stood there looking up
into the high seat of the forklift and scuffed my feet
and at 16 years old I had the right answer: *yes sir*
and so got straight to work sweeping up garbage,
stacking hours, stacking boards up for the neat
presentation the boss was always getting
in my face about. I let my back burn
dark in the sun and my blond hair turn almost white
and my blue eyes tear up in the glare. I breathed
diesel fumes and Atlantic wind, plotted escape.
At morning break I got in the back of the line at the coffee truck
then skulked in the cool shadows of the cement shed
where the crew busted my stones. I just laughed,
flashed the white teeth of my smile, rolled my big eyes.
I wasn't old enough or angry enough yet to fight back
alone but wished that I could get Gerald Parker
down to the yard to straighten those good ol' boys out—
not with his considerable eloquence—
but with his powerful blue arms and hands like clubs—
I'd yell: "Hey boss, here's a *real nigger* for you!"—whack!
But that was the summer Gerald ran from a pack of white cops
and got locked up. He wouldn't get out until his wife and job
were gone. Did I learn what it was like to be black that summer?
If I told you *yes sir* I would be like a man
who gets his first whiff of salt air then claims
that he knows all about the ocean, the bizarre pelagic eyes,
the strangling and stinging deaths of the darkness down there—
which would be a lie, but maybe a lie
with just enough bitter hint of truth.

Planting

After work sometimes in the evenings
I brush off the sawdust,
roll down to Bobby's place,
see if he needs a hand.

Behind the church
a freshly harrowed field
ready for planting
stretches away from the village
all the way to the graveyard.

I sit on the transplanter
mounted on the three-point hitch,
grab greenhouse plants from the baskets,
set them in discs
that turn and push into the dark soil.

Lurch of the tractor, drum-tap sputtering—
we track invisible lines anchored
by distant headstones.
It takes forever to get a row done—
I think the tomatoes will have grown and ripened
by the time we get to the other end.

Or sometimes I walk behind
straightening and firming loose plants.
This is no tender craft:
1200 tomatoes, 2000 peppers, 1500 squash.

In the distance the highway hums.
The church bells clang and ring in the night air,
and, without even a hint of God for me now,
sing a song of everything

just as it is: dirt-caked palms,
tired back, choke-fired truck engine,
the dark road rising toward thick stars,
then down the hill and home.

The Foreman Calls in Sick

We had no idea what to do—without a boss
our years of experience in lumber disappeared
like a penny in a slick magician's hand.

I got nowhere
        fast
holding the broom by the bristle end
tapping the handle along the concrete
        like Charlie Chaplin looking
for trouble.

Phil and Mike tried the forklifts for awhile,
but decided that they were too dangerous,
so they parked them and took the keys:
left them standing
        greasy, rusting monuments
masts raised in the rain.

By that time, five units of plywood
were splayed out across the lot
like playing cards.

Customers drove away, never to return!

Spencer got lost trying to decode swirly grains.
He mixed up the maple and the oak,
the spruce and pine. Soon,
the orders were a mess, and the drivers
gave up and started to deliver whatever-the-hell.
Now, I'm afraid
things went too far
and somewhere someone is building

a garbage can shed
out of old-growth, clear-heart redwood.

It should stand for a thousand years.

Looking at a Photo of Our Grandfather, Seeing You

for Phil, my twin

Poppy looked back at me
with the exact friendly tilt of your head.
His lips were yours suggesting a smile, priming
a wisecrack. Even in fading black and white
his cheek bones were not mine, not Andersen,
but Ferencz—yes, *yours* reflecting
any available light—Great Depression light
or light in the Decade of Greed.

Now, I can think about you on Friday nights
when we were seventeen: scrubbed clean
after work—slick. When I asked
"Where're you going?" you'd just say "out"
before tearing up the driveway

and I see our grandfather
fierce to go, desperate to get off the homestead,
lurching away in some old flivver,
banging gears with abandon
up the Boston Post Road.

I burst out again laughing
at how you transformed
cartoon-like into our cigar-chomping boss—
a squawking impression that doubled me up
so hard I thought I had a hernia.
Some of the other guys, helpless on the slab,
begged you to stop

and I can join Poppy's four brothers and three sisters
howling, falling all around the cherry tree
as he aped old man Johnson loping home.

I think of Poppy's sister Sophie after his funeral
crying: "Oh, Fran always watched out for us"

and I can hear your phone calls every week,
checking in on me, your unabashed "I love you"
on my answering machine.

In our love that sometimes felt like hate,
in how you or I would drop kick the basketball,
clear the way to pummel each other
into the hard pack behind the old summer kitchen,
I recognize the two-fisted loyalty
of Poppy giving it back twice as hard
to the bully twice his size
who dared to pick on his younger brother,
and then turning to box the little boy's ears
for having taunted the oaf like a fool.

Yes, now I picture
our grandfather in 1928—
framing a new little room on the house
in which we'd grow up too:
he's proud of the home taking shape
with chestnut boards hewn from the mill,
but also desirous, needing to look forward
to something besides endless labor

and I can understand you in 1988—exhausted and pissed,
helping our father frame an equipment shed out back
with twisted lumber you'd salvaged from work,
swinging the hammer, caroming wide
but striking down true, driving
and driving the spikes home
as if maybe there was something that needed to be killed
as well as built.

From Spencer to Lisa

OK, you can come back home now. Sorry. I just got a little hot
under the collar like my father used to say. ~~But what's wrong~~
~~with you?~~ No…. scratch that. Hey, I fixed the window.
You know I'd never hit you or anything, right? Sweeping up
the glass I thought about how you'd probably take the shards
and turn them into art. I always think about stuff sweeping.
This morning at work, pushing my broom alone, a little high,
I saw (no pun—ha ha) how new pine boards in gray weathered racks
shine. Then I got it. That's how you probably look next to me.
Go ahead and put something beautiful next to something not-so-
-beautiful and see what happens. Today I ate lunch at the pizza house
by the tracks on the shore. That crazy old man who hits golf balls
down the sidewalk came in, had a roast beef grinder, like me.
When I got home I was busting to do something, but Lis,
there's nothing to do. So I pedaled out here past the shops
and past the cottages and laid out my sleeping bag on the beach.
God, I hope you're not with him….what am I doing? I'm freezing
my butt off out here ! What would you think if you could
suddenly see me, the power plant glow rippling out across
the black bay to me? ~~Baby, I'm like a spent fuel rod.~~ Today
I asked Andersen what I should write since he thinks he's a poet
and he told me to write about when I fell in love with you.
Well you probably already know it. Nine years ago driving
you and your big ugly brothers home from the Thanksgiving game
in your pop's Pontiac Grand Prix you sang to the radio, you
let your long brown hair spill down over your small shoulders
and pressed against me a little. I could smell you.

Lisa's Reply

Oh, Spence, I got your letter and I'm so proud of you for saying
what you *feel* for once, I really am. It's funny that you were at the beach
when you were writing to me because most of the time I'm right here
on my aunt's plush glassed-in patio looking out at the light and water
changing on the Sound, just laying on the sofa reading tons of books
from her shelves. Some are brand new and others are so old and brittle
I have to hold them like little birds. No, I'm not with *him*—it's the books
I'm in love with now. I think maybe I need to get back to school. Hon,
I read Hemingway, and I thought about how sad your anger seems
when you drink sometimes. And a book about Mary Wollstencraft,
who survived her father's fury to stand up for all women (and men!)
I remembered when *I* fell in love with *you*: that night you tore me away
from Daddy's drunken rage. Things change. I put it back up on the shelf
and realized just how tired I've become of saving you from yourself.

The Rustic Café

Permittees: Francis and Victoria Ferencz

I. Courage

"You don't have the balls!"
Spencer heckles me from the back seat
as I accelerate past the town dump and aim
towards Florida, like I'm really going to do it
this time, and my brother Phil shoots back to him:
"You didn't get us any farther down the line last week,
numb nuts," and Spencer smacks him in the back of the head
but knows he's gonna pay for it later.
This is the way history repeats itself every pay day—
out on US Route 1, the three of us
always almost find the courage to just keep driving,
then stop on the edge of town—
Nanny and Poppy's bar.

In the parking lot I say to Spencer:
"You're just afraid of our grandmother."

"She threw a kitchen knife at me, man!"

"She was drunk. Anyway, that means she likes you."

I open the thick door, bells tinkling,
Maximum Occupancy: 27.
Poppy—close to eighty and alive
against all odds, greets us with
a crinkled smile, and white hair:
"Hello, hello—come on, stay awhile,"
steps out from behind the shiny pine bar
he built with his son, shuffles across
the boot-worn, wide plank floor to the TV,

stretches his bent five-foot frame up
to change the channel.

We sit down to Camels and Rolling Rocks—
Nanny serves us the best damn burgers
anybody ever ate, handsome homemade pickles
on the side, and we have the same conversation
about no raises again, how Jeremy'd be better off
if he just stuck to beer like us.

Later, brave and primed for the night,
we get up, and Poppy won't let me pay,
doesn't want to let us go: "Where're yous goin?
No need to hurry off now"—Spencer answers for us:
"Girls, Poppy, girls!"

Before stepping out, I look around:
one young couple sits by the window,
a few old-timers hunch like ghosts in the corners,
"Bud Man" stickers still stick to the bumper pool table,
ancient tools hang from rough-sawn beams,
black and white memories hang on the walls.

II. Power

My brother and I looking like gangly fawns
folded up against the legs of our parents
beneath the bar table and singing with the jukebox,
pretending the beer coasters are banjos, watching
        Mr. Jeffers who strums
and stumbles his way between the drunk,
packed, loving, laughing, singing crowd while Joe
makes coins disappear and reappear behind Sophie's ears,
and Shirley plays with Charley, the beer-drinking, clowning crow
        who squawks: "Shit! Fuck! Goddamn!"

and Captain, the ex-gigolo whose wife didn't
leave him a cent,
argues with Nick about his tomatoes and rabbits
and Happy Jennings brags about the incredible
    power
of his '57 Chevy—"Last Stop Before Hell"
painted on the hood.

III. Need

Little Vicky, blond hair in curlers,
in her pink dress and ready to go now,
picks up the toppled bar stool
and begins to speak to Big Vicky:

"Come on, Ma—get up!
I put on the dress you made me!
Come on, now Ma—you promised!"
then whining a little, pleading

"Come on, Ma, please....
I'll do your hair!
Get up, get up, get up...."

IV. Testimony

Nanny sits down next to me
on the beer-stained church pew, smoke
curling around us, she hands me a card—
"I don't know who this is—Poppy can't remember, either,
but ain't it sweet and nice...":

December 14, 1987
Sarasota, Florida
Dear Francis and Victoria: Merry Christmas! I was thinking

lately about the big old place before the fire and how many nice
meals we had and so many laughs. I remember how even after
closing time, you'd have us walk back down the house and we'd
drink and laugh and play cards until sunrise next morning. And
your beautiful kids. Must be all grown up! And Vick, you would
even cook meals for the hobos—white or colored or what have
you —and Fran, you would set them up some nights in the cabin.
Last night on TV they called the 1950s golden years, but seemed
like hard times for a lot of us too. Jesus takes note of good people
like you, where have all the good people gone.
God bless you and yours,
Jean Mulcahy

V. Rage

Bleary-eyed, home from grad school, I see the place
shut down again—decide to stop and see what's
what. My eyes adjust to streetlight-smeared
dark: empty whiskey and vodka bottles on the bar.

Poppy's curled up on the pew under
a tattered, cigarette-burned table cloth.
It's freezing. He's out cold, blood
caked around his ears, left eye blackened.
They fought, and he let her win,
offered himself up again.

I find her in the back hallway, face
down, one leg propping open the ladies' restroom
door, as if she planned to release the blue florescent light
that bathes her. She's not dead. She's sleeping
like a baby. I kneel over her, hands shaking
with rage as I think of my defeated grandfather,
these ruins, and my mother terror-struck at five,
watching scenes like this unfold, always
believing that she could make it right somehow.

It would be so easy to kill this woman,
this beast. Just drag her down to the brook, empty
the cash register. It should have been done
years ago. The time is right, I turn her over,

but she starts to moan a little as I drag her great weight,
and I only make it a little way down the hall,
where I stop, slump against the cigarette machine.
I look down: her hair is still black, long and flowing—
in this light, this dark, her skin is smooth, her body
unburdened. She could be twenty years old again;

a moment ago she could have been telling a joke or falling
in love with her husband. She could have been standing
in her swimsuit on the sun-drenched stone dam up on Powers' Lake,
where she made the farm boys forget Depression and ache
with desire. She could have just slipped beneath the water
and pushed out away from shore, lithe and exuberant, legs
kicking, arms reaching and stroking, her whole life before her.

VI. Envoi

I release this poem

as a kind of surrender,
the way Poppy stopped taking his heart
medicine, poured one last shot
for himself and one for his wife,
handed it to her, walked back
to his bedroom and dropped.

I release this poem
as a kind of triumph—
the way Nanny lived on because Little Vicky
got her out of the Rustic at last, or

25

the way she stayed sober those last eight years,
after half a century of violent binges.

I release this poem now
the way my mother—kind woman—
released her mother from final, useless struggle—

with a soothing voice,
a sweet, merciful lie:
"You can go, you can go,
you've made everything all right."

II.

The Trails

Postcard from Chimney Pond

Climbed the talus around the pond last night—so many pebbles
around a puddle from the views of Baxter Peak, but down here
chunks of granite as big as the small house I grew up in, all
jumbled, jutting out of cold, clear water and piled up towards
the stars. Silent lightning split the sky far north. Scrambled
as far up the rock throat as I safely could and then some.
Slept beneath the cliffs. Had a dream of you so real that
for a long time after waking up, it felt good to have seen you again.

Cathedral Trail

*I was deep within the hostile ranks of clouds, and all objects were
obscured by them. Now the wind would blow out a yard of clear
sunlight....* — Thoreau, *Ktaadn*

Clink and *thunk* of steel bars,
the relentless underscore of wind rushes
massive as a wall against our ears
and snaps our parkas.

Into it
eight voices rise: *HEAVE!*

A granite boulder, lichen-slick, wrested
from its nest of stone, stands straight up
for a moment—free of our levering
then thuds and smacks
(gun powder smell) tumbles
like a billiard ball

to rest
having come farther in five seconds
than it had in twelve thousand years.

Margaret drops her hard hat, drops
down to scoop it back up, looks up
to catch and hold my gaze

before clouds sock us in again, soak us
all through lunch—in moments parting
from distant thin brown trails winding across the tableland,
disappearing up over the North Peaks

and around the rim of the Northwest Basin:
brief glimpses
of all the places she and I might go to be alone

and all the work to be done!

Trail Crew, Baxter Park

Margaret, Yvonne, Ailsa, Tom, Nick, Liz, Lester
and I pack in chain saws and wire rope,
plunge our hands into freezing streams,
haul up stones, build timber bridges, take turns
patrolling the mountain alone
high above Chimney Pond. Exhausted,
we return finally to sleep huddled
in tool sheds and rain-slapped tents.

I wonder about the trail that brought me here.

In the interest of lightness
we have all left things behind—
I left my good friend Jeremy dope sick
in a chair in New London, Connecticut
because I had looked into the gray mask
of his face and believed
I had not tried hard or soon enough
to save him. Before the needle

when he was well, he loved people
and mountains. Able to win anyone
with his big open greetings—warm
and glowing in any wind chill factor,
he tape recorded conversations
with strangers standing braced on open summits
or stopped along steep switchbacks.

Back in his cramped apartment, we would sit
at kitchen table and listen to those voices
tell bad jokes and talk about the hard miles down
to trail head or whom they missed most of all—
always the rush of wind or patter of White
Mountain rain as music behind their words.

Now I imagine him in his slicker:
hollering to me from up the trail or plunging
out of the brush into the path at last, roaring with joy
and clutching his compass like a talisman.
Or finding us here in the warm cabin at Russell Pond;
he'd let himself in to cook us dinner,
talk politics with Margaret and Tom, stay up late
reading by gas light. But he was gone
before I stumbled across this place
and found a home for him too late.

A Brief Note from Spencer

Hey—I don't like to write but you wrote so
I guess I got to send something back.
I can really picture the mountains—not my thing,
but it sounds like you got it made: all those trees
and streams and mountain lakes and Margaret
sounds like a gift of nature, too. Listen—
don't worry but my Dad checked himself into
the VA hospital—guess he was ready to end it
but thought he'd give himself one last chance.
It's got me shook up cause he's been mostly proud
and pissed for the 25 years I've known him—I mean,
he could be down, but this! We went to see him
and let me tell you that big old power plant
has been decommissioned. He looks smaller
somehow—just sits there crying all the time.
I let Ma talk to him, but I had to go out to the parking lot
for a smoke, and you want to hear something weird?
Remember how his buddies at *The Boat* gave him
the name "War Hawk"? Well I'm leaning against the truck
puffing away and this red-tail comes swooping down,
screeching and circling and I'm looking it right in the eyes
and then it takes off fighting the wind.
That's got to be a good sign, right? I swear
I'm not shitting you. Anyways, we'll see you this winter—
I'm still not drinking, Lisa's back and says hi,
everyone misses you but I don't that much.

Dream

I was rapping on the door
of your mountain house,
the aurora borealis shook impatiently,
sprung against the sky.
My teeth chattered—as gray and cold
as Katahdin above treeline.
You finally opened up:
    There I was, holding the door
    waiting for Bertolt Brecht
    to come in from admiring the trees.
    There was a black lab—blind and friendly.
    A woman in nineteenth century dress
    who, we all agreed, was very beautiful
    (even the trees lined up along her path
        (her little footsteps on black matted
        leaves of the forest floor)).
    I swear that was Dorothy Day shuffling
    past the pot-bellied stove
    clutching an infant deeply in her arms.
    The rest of us had no famous names—
    there must have been twenty of us,
    some yellow, red,
    black and blue, strung out,
    stomping and crying from war.
We all came in and had some soup.
I know that you were angry at first
but the next day we had work for everyone
in the bright valley, with all the food!

Saddle Trail to Tableland

Like work and peace, comrades/ joy, too, is revolutionary
—Roque Dalton

I swept the cabin clean at Chimney Pond,
balanced the weight in my backpack, then locked
the door, looked up, and chose the Saddle Trail—

more slide than trail—I climbed a thousand feet
in altitude, gained step by careful step,
granite and gravel, sky and twisted trees.

I topped off at the tableland. The wind
was sheer enough to scrape and blow the lies
straight from my swollen soul. See, I had run

from jobs and joblessness—I wasn't going
back. Or was, and stood there so afraid.
I looked to distant Canada and south

to endless lakes. The state of Maine stretched out
before me: blue and green, and dark and light.
I stepped around arctic cushions, Labrador Tea,

wind-stunted spruces no higher than my knees.
It's funny now, but in that howling place
I chose a rock and sat. I ate some lunch;

I bundled up and breathed. I think that I
believed that stone, and wind, and storms, and ponds
of glacial melt could help me face the world.

An older couple came strolling out of clouds.
They waved as if I lived next door and we
were meeting in their garden. I waved back

and watched them holding hands and moving on,
as bright as beacons in their ragged gear—
they flapped like joyful flags far up the trail.

So I looked north to Canada and south
to endless lakes. I bundled up and breathed,
and dreamed of girlfriends, finding honest work

and peace, and planned some ways of growing old.

To An Old Friend, from Good Earth Farm

Your letter tastes of boulder ice
and sky, tells me how you keep
bouncing from mountain trail crews
to work in town, and I think how it's wonderful
to wander like Han Shan or Kerouac
defying the regime from a distance!

Wonderful and not. I mean
we can't just be about finding a place
where there's no through-trail.
I used to think I could disappear, but I can't.
Even if no one ever hears from us again
every inch of the Earth is mapped by satellite.

You think you're decaying heroically
into the pine needles and roots and moss
and changing light of the forest
when the bulldozers come to seal off your bones
forever in a mall.

Back here, you can at least put up a fight.
I'm not saying to not go out into
those deep valleys of rock, aching cold streams
and ancient growth. Go

to find true loneliness, to feel
the pulse of wilderness, go
to grow tired of yourself
and to find your way back again.

July: Good Earth Farm

With the light just beginning
to seep into the valley, I step out;
the tractor sputters, warms
to the work of the day. Mist chases mist,
rolls and sweeps off the south-sloping pasture
back to the shadows of esker woods.
By noon, the firmament runs from blue to blue,
and the whole Earth seems to sink into the Sun.
Mike, Lesley, Dan and I harvest for hours, wilt,
take quick breaks in the shade
between trips to the walk-in with filled truck
and tractor cart. Back in the fields
between turnips and beets
we tell jokes, argue about *The Good Life.*

Every afternoon
I stand and watch the same flock
of sparrows return in the same pattern
to cottonwoods rattling in the breeze.

Life is so beautiful here!
You know, at supper this evening
reading the paper at the kitchen table
sitting in the old bus seat torn from the back
of the market van,
I almost missed
the story on page three:

"Children Set Homeless Man on Fire"

"Children Set Homeless Man on Fire"

I can't shake that story in the *Globe* the whole next day. Lesley
laughs at me as I start to carry basil into the walk-in: *What are
you so spaced about?* And I don't want to talk about it. I
transplant lettuce plugs to the ends of crooked rows and sit,
forgetting where I am. Could Crazy Charlie have been the one?
Have I seen these kids at market? Why the hell wasn't this a
front page story? At night, in my barn room, I stay up late
reading some hip Zen, *Sports Illustrated*, a Marxist dialectic
and finally fall asleep:

> my childhood buddies and I
> are thirteen again, middle-schoolers
> on the sidewalk, not far from the Cambridge Square Market—
> I pour gasoline into a heap of blanket
>   and bone, and one of them lights a match
> suddenly aflame
>   I am the one leaping up from the street,
> shrieking, I see their faces laugh and laugh…

before I explode awake.

Moonlight. Concrete walls. Blue glass candleholders.

I find my boots at the end of their tracks
    and step out into the night
the wind whispers against my cheeks
the grasses rush toward death
as I hunker down, clenched and shaking like a fist,
then stand
        spread open
            to nameless constellations
at once at one with
    and torn from this life.

October: Good Earth Farm

Against the cold, I stuff holes with t-shirts and feathers,
crawl back into bed and try to sleep.
October already and this barn room—
    a 12 x 14 concrete block addition—
will be home for another month
before we three farm hands (lost
college kids, really) move on
to New York City, Guatemala, Willimantic.

I keep thinking of Will Johnson
who lost his farm two years ago
and how just the other night
his wife found him sitting in the bathtub at 1 a.m.
shotgun loaded and ready on the linoleum floor.
I was told he grabbed the gun quick,
took her hours to coax him out
pleading and crying with him. Now
that old farmer, who at eighty still
threw bales with us under this summer's spreading sky,
sits in a room with barred windows
and doors locked from the outside.

I try to really see and hold these scenes, but
keep slipping to Will in shafts of hay loft light—
still muscled, chaff sticking to sweat-glazed arms.
I want to ask him for wisdom,
want him to tell me how he got so broken and sad.
He just smiles and says once again
Bugs? Plant your potatoes a little later than usual
and *My granddaddy could've taught you about organic*
and *Better watch out—where there's money, there's cheating.*

Postcard from New York City: May 1994

here I am at the global capital of global capital....
see the towers gleam and thrust up into blue sky (the picture
lies—the sky's more gray than blue). Rosa tells me
her mother works cleaning guys' offices and desks
on the top floors. Someday, buddy, our great-great grandchildren
will take these babies down—very carefully, gently even, piece
by piece, working together, they'll ship out the windows
to be used on cold frames in ten thousand winter gardens

As I Went Walking

away from the dispersing May Day crowd
    on the New Haven Green, one big
    wandering woman gave me a hug
    I glowed for a week;

out past Pike Place Market I witnessed
    a young man screaming from
    some burning focus in his brain or soul
    towards the icy peaks that cut
    into sky above Puget Sound
    and haunt the city of Seattle;

up from the far fields with a friend
    after harvesting and hoeing,
    a hard, delicious rain caught us
    laughing and soaked
    fifty yards from the barn;

like a man away from the bus stop in Boston
    where Ailsa said goodbye
    my throat caught a bit, but
    I was tall and hungry
    and full of breath;

down Main Street on lunch break
    I ducked at the crack of gunshots
    but it was a transformer exploding above me
    sending up lightning, smoke, fire at noon
    and my heart pounding like traffic;

towards a battered old station wagon
    husband, wife, kids stuffed
    in blankets and sleeping bags,
    a sign in the window:

Will Trade Stuff For Gas
my gut clenched like a fist
for their resilience and fear;

waist deep in the duff, clambering
    for a solid step, following
    a bearing out of a high country col
    a voice came sounding from
    all around me:

this land belongs to us
    not as the business
    belongs to its owner
    but as a mother belongs to her children
    as a hunter belongs to the tracks
    as the future belongs to those
    willing to sing through, kick at
    one of a million tangled ways
    into it

White Mountain Poem

We leave the car with our bellies
still full of pancakes and coffee
to struggle through the first miles
of low country. Our shoulders take to the weight—
our legs to the trail. We find white-tail tracks
deep and splayed in spring mud.
That afternoon, we stop at white water bursting
above our heads, slamming
at our feet — I watch the mist
and color spectrum hang over you
as you bend to fill a bottle.
Up higher, tortured firs yield to one trail.
On a bald summit we lay out
our bags. The blue land below
occasionally glints with an automobile
or opens to pasture
and eventually is draped in black
as the Earth continues to spin
its heat and light into space.
We zip up, press shoulders.
We whisper and laugh.
We're sitting in the stars.

III.

The Real World

You Must

You must have a hope
that will let you stomp and sing
at any cold dawn.
You must not wait
to love the student who loves you
and would like to kill you.
You must read the story again
and again to the child
who receives you with a bovine stare.
You must get up
every day to punch in
not dreaming on transcendence,
not desiring new heroes or gods,
not looking the other way,
but looking for the other way
and ready to talk to everyone on the line.
You must not wait
for official approval
nor general consensus
to rage. You must
come again to kneel
in shiny, rock-strewn soil
not to pray, but to plant.
Yes, even now
as ice caps melt and black top
goes soft in the sun
you must prepare for the harvest.

Encounter

Think back, now, remember
that dirty bag of a man
you tripped over on the sidewalk
when you looked down
the first time
you did not see a *wino* or *bum*
but someone
who had been to high school
someone
who knew how to stand in lines
and wanted to love his neighbor

for weeks at night
trying to sleep
all you could see were his eyes
pavement blue   one
looking the other way

True Story

I traveled dreamscape to Washington, D.C.
to join a demonstration and stood
with a 12-foot-tall, sad-faced man who wore tattered
canvas chaps outside the Pentagon where
we sang *We Shall Overcome* mournfully
off-key until the black-clad storm troopers
came cracking heads open, and someone
shoved me into a shack by the ice-clogged Potomac.
Jack Kerouac and Gary Snyder sat sifting through the broken ear
drums of sparrows but Pete Seeger greeted me with a firm handshake
saying "Hello, Jon—Woody said you'd be coming."
Of course, that's not what he really said

when wide awake I met him two weeks later.
Twenty-five with friends and girlfriends strewn across
the continent, relentless pain in my back, working
as a long-term substitute teacher with working poor
suicidal youth but getting paid as a tutor,
no benefits, putting in weekends for my parents'
failing landscape business, sad as the moon and living
at home again, I took my dream as a sign and drove I-95
South to Wilbur Cross High School in New Haven, Connecticut
to hear Pete Seeger play a benefit concert for striking Yale workers.
I arrived early and found all doors locked or chained but one
I slipped through and then down dark hallways to the boys' room
in back of the auditorium, where I stood at a urinal
suddenly hearing the unmistakable lilting voice
of the great folk singer next door. When I was done
I shyly entered the room where a dozen big women
with friendly faces and all wearing union buttons sat around a table
folding programs and one told me to come in and Pete
Seeger himself looking a little gaunt in his green sweater and red
shirt but eyes as cheerful as in my dream waved me over to sit

on a folding chair beside him as he plucked his banjo and practiced but
not so much as to strain his aging voice. He gave me a short history
of the labor movement and sang a miners' song
and I got up the nerve to ask him if he had read Agnes Smedley's
Daughter of Earth, in which the bosses seal up the mine
to snuff out a fire and snuff out the miners in the process
as their wives drop hysterical at the shaft entrances and at the feet
of machine-gun armed Pinkerton goons. He said no but his wife's mother

had known Agnes back in the early 20s as a great revolutionary
and one heck of a fiery speaker. When he asked me what I did,
and I told him that I was a high school English teacher,
he stopped strumming, turned to me and said:
"Well, Jon, it seems to me that your job is to teach kids
to read between the lines."

F.Y.I.

If you walk into the kitchen
and I'm bent over with my head stuck in the oven
baby, don't worry—
I'm just warming up
to write you a poem

If I disappear with a .44 revolver
into the Sierras, wait
for me to reappear, startle you
on a sidewalk in Connecticut with
the thud, the thud in your ears
the thud of my new animal heart

If I wave and call
"hallo" to you from a clinging perch
on a bridge in Minneapolis,
don't try to reason me down
before I've drunk in the entire landscape, the river
pouring itself into the burning
ball we lose every day to find again

If I ever load my revolver,
it will be because I am defending us
with a tender rage, because
I love my life, and peace,
and I want to feel
        like *the cloud in trousers*

and if you see me raising
that gun to my head, it's only a nightmare,
        so scream
            boltwideawake, find me—
eyes closed, breathing beside you in bed

If you discover me in the garage
curled up in the idling car, well
I've drifted off on a repair that took too long,
so for godssakes open the windows! Stick
my face in the snow! Wake me up
so I can tell you the truth
that the dead know

Hey, Baby

We lie down on Sunday afternoon,
my head on her stomach. I
tap a code, then a beat, sing
top 40 and lullabies,
try to reach you in your
warm, dark, watery, tight world:
hey baby, hey baby,
will you hear your father's voice?
You kick a little, I see you
stretch against the soft boundary, feel
what must be your tiny fist press against my cheek.

I've searched my old and present beliefs
to fathom this:
Are you one of God's miracles?
Are you waiting to be pushed out
into the hero journey?
Are you returning to try again for Nirvana?
Are you a refugee from Plato's cave
who will enter and be blinded by the true world?
Or will you come struggling,
ready to change the world to know it?

All three of us fall asleep
as light-dappled shadows grow
into the afternoon.

Love in Willimantic

I.
Summer, and all the windows
of Hotel Hooker open wide to furnished rooms,
the collective hum and click
of oscillating fans, men and women
with faces hardened by struggle
or surrender. You and I
find each other living happily
in an old boss's house on the hill.

II.
In autumn the green curtain burns
brilliantly for a moment before dropping,
spreading and fading across the street
like news or time or light.
I have been meaning to tell you:
at night, as you sleep,
the stars rotate through the chilled air
into our bedroom,
landing silently on the floor,
in your hair, nestling in the blankets
as you breathe.

III.
One winter night, we're hit so hard
the next day's a certain snow day.
Outside, there are no streets—
only a muffled landscape of drifts against buildings,
one bunch of kids whooping
under yellow light and blazing flakes.

We trudge downtown and out across the footbridge,
first over the rail yard of buried timbers
and flatcars loaded with snow,

then out farther, higher still above the river:
black limbs bent down
to the black water relentlessly carving out,
running under a geography of ice, great chunks
like buoyant boulders breaking off,
colliding and rolling, clogging up at the bend.
We could fool ourselves into believing
that the whole world might change
as we stand watching—warm and quiet.

IV.
Spring, and Hosmer Mountain
is green again,
green as rain—dark green, too—
cool as a pocket of river air.
The future is either here
or somewhere out there.

Either way, love,
I delight in how we circle back to this season
when even the streets break out in blossom
and nothing is left unborn.

Learn, My Boy

I sit in Bud's Café having breakfast
(Georgia's yelling at her customers who love her
cooking and abuse)
and eavesdrop on an old-timer's ghost story....
How one night shift at the old mill he watched
a cheerful, dapper man,
dressed in coat with tails and top-hat
just stroll down the empty hall:
I swear to God
he looked like some big owner
or industrialist from the nineteenth century
just walkin' around like he still owned the place....

I imagine the ghost of Mr. Orwell Fullerton,
dead now ninety years, slip
down Milk Street past
souped-up and lowered Datsuns
where men hang in shadows on the stoops,
and three children, all on one bicycle, arms flailing,
bounce down the sidewalk, riotously
laughing in the shadows of the Thread City mill houses.

I read that in 1837 Fullerton's father told him
never forfeit the opportunity to learn, my boy
and I guess maybe he learns now
    to speak a little Spanish
    to move to merengue
    and, too late,
    to hate that boss's life he lived.

My Mother Paints Again

Her first attempt in decades—
a gift for my wife and me—
a watercolor, still-life
hangs in our kitchen:

three ears of corn in a basket,
two husks torn back, revealing
milky, plump kernels.

I grieve
    for so much left unpainted:

rudbeccia, tall and stalky, spreading
and blooming up out of hard pack gravel driveway—
oranges, yellows, reds
    as varied and flickering in the wind
  as flame

or the sudden face of a lynx
    perched in the mist on an old stone wall
in the twisting, early morning farm road drive

to the small red brick school where she cooked hot meals for years

and watched over children who needed her,
like pink-cheeked second grader Mary Coombs,
whose love
was not quite yet snuffed out by the dazed mommy
that filled her moldy thermos with beer.

Or abstract-expressionist works:
    audacious strokes of violent
        black against radiant schemes and looping green

swirls with titles like "Self-Portrait: Sis, 1962" or
"Divorce After Three Decades: Three Weeks In."

And mixed-media pieces in cardboard, canvas, old
utensils and electric light. Anything. But mostly
anything with hope, anything that assumes a future,
or reminds us that grief
        is an easy posture, a slippery emotion,

not worthy of this work that hangs in my kitchen, this still-
life that moves with butter melting in summer heat
and crooked, old-fashioned rows of bursting kernels—
some for food, some for seed, enough to live on
not just today
        but also tomorrow.

The Daughter I Never Had

Laura, seventeen, dark hair and brilliant smile,
student in my creative writing class,
tells me just before last bell
about her dream:
she walked into the cabin at Walden Pond
and found my baby boy there,
in the bed next to the crackling fireplace,
wrapped in a wool blanket and giving her
his big, gummy grin.
She took him out to the pond
after buying him some snugglies at the gift shop
and held him while ice skating—he giggled
and laughed as she did loops and spins.
When she got back to the cabin, she realized
this is my brother,
which in turn makes me realize
I'm her dad.

The Real World

What are you going to do when you get out into the real world?
    —often asked of students by teachers in America's high schools

This is the real world.

Or at least this is one world, as real
as any world, more brutal than some, far
less brutal than others,

                    but real.

Given the resources, I could prove it:
    some kind of metaphysical tape measure
strung out and flopping in the space and time between
my B period class and my F period class
would show them to be as distant from one another
as any two randomly chosen moons
                    or their own neighborhoods.

You might counter and say that 93% of our school
population is white and that's not the real world, but I also might say
that many of those kids will marry white partners and have
white children and live in white neighborhoods with white fences,
and they will say that they earned their place in society and no one
is to blame and blacks have to earn their way like anyone
else but don't get them wrong they're not racist, and we should
be *tolerant* of everyone, even if they're poor as the dim light
of Laundromats or rich as the blue light of swimming pools.

I gather anecdotal evidence, too.
Walking down these halls, I see every
face as somehow my own reflection—distorted,
                    then clarified, given back:

62

There's sixteen-year-old Dusty Gomes
whose post-traumatic stress syndrome is as real
as any Vietnam Veteran's. He'll bloody
a kid up real good, only later willing
to give anything to stop himself.
When he was six, he saw his father
shot to death by the police.
He swears that sometimes at night
he can hear his dad call his name.

And what about Leah Rollins, brilliant and cheerful,
who could be so satisfied with her own award-winning
poetry and art but wants to throw privilege off her back,
flee to Chiapas or Harlem or Tibet,
and stand with the Oppressed if they'll have her?

Don't forget Joseph Shafer, who wandered
these halls as quietly as air and left no wake, save
for the occasional melt down: head on desk, sent back
to my room to get it together—tried to overdose on insulin,
hasn't been here for three months, and not one person, no
one has asked me where he went. Except that I delivered
a get-well card to his house and had a conversation with him
(or as near to a conversation as one could have with him
in his cheerfully glazed-eyed state and strings
of non-sequiturs) I, too, could be convinced he wasn't real.

And there's me. I must be real, with this knot in my gut,
and every now and then exhilaration on days
of breakthrough. I get up in the morning, kiss
my beautiful wife and our beautiful sons,
tiptoe from warm room to warm room, doubting
that I could deserve this Paradise. Unless I do something
stupid or radical, I'll have this job for as long as I want it.
Now, I just have to let my skin harden to the right thickness

in order to stick this out for thirty-something years: thin
enough to want to visit Joey with a card, push Leah
in the right direction, or plead with Dusty to do the next
right thing, but not so thin that I'd let the thousands
of lives that flow past like canyon-carving rapids
carry me away. Not that thin.

Two Mottos

For the CEO, the boy
who grew muscles riding rambunctious horses
over Litchfield Hills and became the man
to fill his Daddy's shoes:

I got mine
     and I got yours too

For the student, the injured
worker who reads in the flickering light
of the community college lobby and hears
the security guard tell him "Time to go home, buddy"
just as he used to hear bartenders announce last call:

Wherever something is illuminated
something also burns

Soldier

In the bustle of passing time,
I do not recognize you
filling up the frame of my classroom door
in full-dress uniform, your chiseled jaw

and wall of a chest, only your smirk
seems familiar—then, shocked recognition:
Michael! I want to salute but shake your hand,
instead. While sophomore girls giggle and gawk,

we chat, catch up, and I venture
a critical thought about the war.
Unruffled and almost condescendingly
you tell me that *policy is for politicians,*

that you can disassemble/assemble/fire any rifle,
self-extract from a mine field, call
in an air strike, lead an ambush, execute
and shout out orders like a machine.

After the job is done, you say
you won't be a loser like your old man
who *threw dinks out of Hueys*
but got his ass kicked by their ghosts

thirty years later. I cough and change
the subject. We laugh about your record-breaking
string of detentions, and I remember how
you used to come to see me—a scrawny,

wounded, angry boy, missing your mother
who fled, or bringing poetry only for me, or
in trouble for leaving a note posted
on your tormentor's locker, threatening

to kill him. Now you calmly tell me
"Mr. Andersen, I just wanted to thank you
for your support during tough personal times,"
and almost overwhelmed by the urge

to shake you, scream in your face:
"Look! See how you bought their shit—
how you let them go and make another soldier
where a man might have been?"

I let myself half-salute, slap you on the shoulder,
and at the final bell dismiss you,
one tough guy to another:
"Hey, Mike—just come home to us alive."

Spencer Goes to School

I'm surprised as hell
at how I get a little sick in the stomach
as soon as I pull the truck into the lot—
I've got a load of sheetrock for the high school's
new addition, and seeing this place makes me feel like
that fifteen-year-old skinny bag of nerves again,
wiping his nose on his sleeve and hiding
a hard-on before first bell.

Then I flex my biceps and start to laugh—
I'll go find Andersen that bastard and shake him
up a bit. He and his brother and their big words,
thinking they're so smart.
I pass a room marked "Mr. Berry"—
that guy's not dead? I bet I could drop him just by
showing up at his door this morning.
I hurry down the halls like a freshman—
this place has gotten huge—and what these girls wear!
How does anyone get anything done?

I find him standing in front of a class
on the second floor. I consider a surprise guest lecture
about the night Mr. Honorable Andersen had ten
too many at that honky-tonk dive on the Point,
and woke up the next morning
in a puddle of drool on my apartment floor.

But I think maybe that'd go too far, and I never
was one for oral reports anyways. So I flip
him off from the window until he sees me,
and by the shocked, angry flash in his eyes,
I know that for a moment he wants to tell me
to get the hell out of there, but catches himself.

It's weird, me and him, old buddies
now on opposite sides of this glass—
suddenly I feel a little stupid, or old or something.

He gets red, turns away,
and ignores me until I have to give up.
That shit, who does he think he's fooling?
He's still a screw-up like me,
and when I get the chance
I'm gonna ask him if he knows it.

Spring, Catskill Mountains

In April I set out with my father,
lugging his great sluggish heart
and my eight-year-old stepson,
clutching his sharpened stick, to huff up through snow
into hemlocks and shadbush. We step and step
and drop, get up, our laughter falls
down through forest into the valley.
We stop where we guess the brook must run,
crouch down together. Our breathing slows
as we finally hear the dark, murmuring tune,
listen to the water churn and roil,
hidden beneath the snow.

Pit Bull

The pit bull lunges against its leash, lunges
again for my little boy as I scoop him
high up into the safety of my arms.
I stand there on the sidewalk
in front of the city preschool
and bore my eyes into the eyes
of this smirking, strutting twentysomething
who pulls at the other end of the taut chain.
He continues down the street, looks back
once before disappearing out of view
to find me still glaring.

My hope for the brilliant autumn morning
was to finish a poem about teaching peace
and worker solidarity, but in this moment
I am gripped
with a new plan: I will drop Kit off
in his cozy classroom with homemade play-dough
and frosted cupcakes with candy hearts
and new friends and his pretty teacher
whom he will tell about the funny doggy

then I will go track that jerk down,
grind his grin into the curb, swing his dog
dead against some tree or pole or wall.

I don't.
Instead, I return to my study, log on,
check the news:

global waters rise, worker falls from bridge,
terror threat rises, sperm counts and soldiers
fall, timid questions are raised, a love song
falls from the top forty, unemployment figures

(but not unemployment) falls, rhetoric
rises towards Mars, free trade obstacles fall,
anxiety rises, a boy in Pennsylvania has fallen
down a well, Haiti falls, the boy is raised to cheers
as rates of profit fall

and look up to find the hours have fallen away
and I'm still seething. I rise and go
to pick up my son, and then out the door
where I see that fearful young man—his muscled ball of terror
still straining against its chain—walking back up the street
that rises towards my home and I struggle to remind myself
how quickly maybe only twenty years have fallen away from the day
he was a new human being helplessly crying in someone's arms.

The Deal

Before dawn I hike stone-filled dream roads
under a sky hung with flames,
come across children strewn about craters
and oil fires outside Baghdad. Not lucky enough
to have starved
    they burn.

I'm saved
by morning glow in Willimantic,
where I romp with you,
my joy, my little
blue-eyed toddler Kit Jonathan.
We whirl and spin, you stomp and grin,
wrapped in the stereo's sweet sound

as light flutters in the copper beech across
the street, as the phone is allowed to
ring itself out, as traffic begins to meet
at the intersection.

My heart, my son, let's make a deal right now:
I'll teach you to fight the horror
that seems sure to come our way,
if you teach me to dance.

Soon

Four mornings ago
I stood in the yard
by the busy intersection
and thrilled to see
tiny bulges of earth
where I had scraped and filled
a drill of helianthus seeds.
And three days ago
the seedlings burst through dirt, dirt
still clinging to their primary leaves
folded in and forming
the missile heads
of their violent emergence.

Soon
I will watch them
spread open with soft leaves
that catch rain the way
human arms do, soon
I will watch them bloom
with distinct bright faces
(not one the same)
that—all together—look for the sun.

Jon Andersen was born in 1970 in New London, Connecticut, only a few minutes ahead of his fraternal twin brother Phillip. His mother and father worked nights and weekends to rebuild an old farmhouse in nearby East Lyme that had belonged to his mother's family for a number of generations, and they moved there in 1972. For many years

Photo by Robert Smith

his father, a Vietnam Veteran, was employed as a shipper and truck driver for a fruit and produce company, while his mother worked as a cook in a small elementary school. His parents encouraged spirited political and philosophical conversations around the dinner table, and at an early age he began to think about both the honors and injustices of hard work in America. Andersen attended the University of Connecticut, graduating in 1992 with a B.A. in English and a Concentration in Creative Writing. He worked variously as a lumberyard employee, landscape laborer, mountain trail crew member, farmhand, and warehouse worker, among other occupations, before earning secondary English teaching certification from Central Connecticut State University and special education certification from Southern Connecticut State University. Currently, he teaches at E.O. Smith High School in Storrs, Connecticut and lives in what he calls "the beautiful and struggling little city of Willimantic." His poetry has appeared in a number of periodicals, including *Blue Collar Review, The Cafe Review, Connecticut Review, The Haight-Ashbury Literary Journal, The Hartford Courant, Pemmican, Poetry Motel,* and *The Progressive,* as well as in the recent Bottom Dog Press anthology *O Taste and See: Food Poems.* He is the recipient of the 2003 Working People's Poetry Award (Partisan Press) and the 2004 People Before Profits Poetry Prize (Burning Bush Books).

CURBSTONE PRESS, INC.

is a non-profit publishing house dedicated to literature that reflects a
commitment to social change, with an emphasis on contemporary writing
from Latino, Latin American and Vietnamese cultures. Curbstone presents
writers who give voice to the unheard in a language that goes beyond
denunciation to celebrate, honor and teach. Curbstone builds bridges
between its writers and the public – from inner-city to rural areas, colleges to
community centers, children to adults. Curbstone seeks out the highest
aesthetic expression of the dedication to human rights and intercultural
understanding: poetry, testimonies, novels, stories,
and children's books.

This mission requires more than just producing books. It requires ensuring
that as many people as possible learn about these books and read them. To
achieve this, a large portion of Curbstone's schedule is dedicated to
arranging tours and programs for its authors, working with public school
and university teachers to enrich curricula, reaching out to underserved
audiences by donating books and conducting readings and community
programs, and promoting discussion in the media. It is only through these
combined efforts that literature can truly make a difference.

Curbstone Press, like all non-profit presses, depends on the support of
individuals, foundations, and government agencies to bring you, the reader,
works of literary merit and social significance which might not find a place
in profit-driven publishing channels, and to bring the authors and their
books into communities across the country. Our sincere thanks to the many
individuals, foundations, and government agencies who have recently
supported this endeavor: Community Foundation of Northeast Connecticut,
Connecticut Commission on Culture & Tourism, Connecticut Humanities
Council, Greater Hartford Arts Council, Hartford Courant Foundation,
Lannan Foundation, National Endowment for the Arts, and the
United Way of the Capital Area.

Please help to support Curbstone's efforts to present the diverse voices and
views that make our culture richer. Tax-deductible donations can be made
by check or credit card to:
Curbstone Press, 321 Jackson Street, Willimantic, CT 06226
phone: (860) 423-5110   fax: (860) 423-9242
www.curbstone.org

IF YOU WOULD LIKE TO BE A MAJOR SPONSOR OF A
CURBSTONE BOOK, PLEASE CONTACT US.